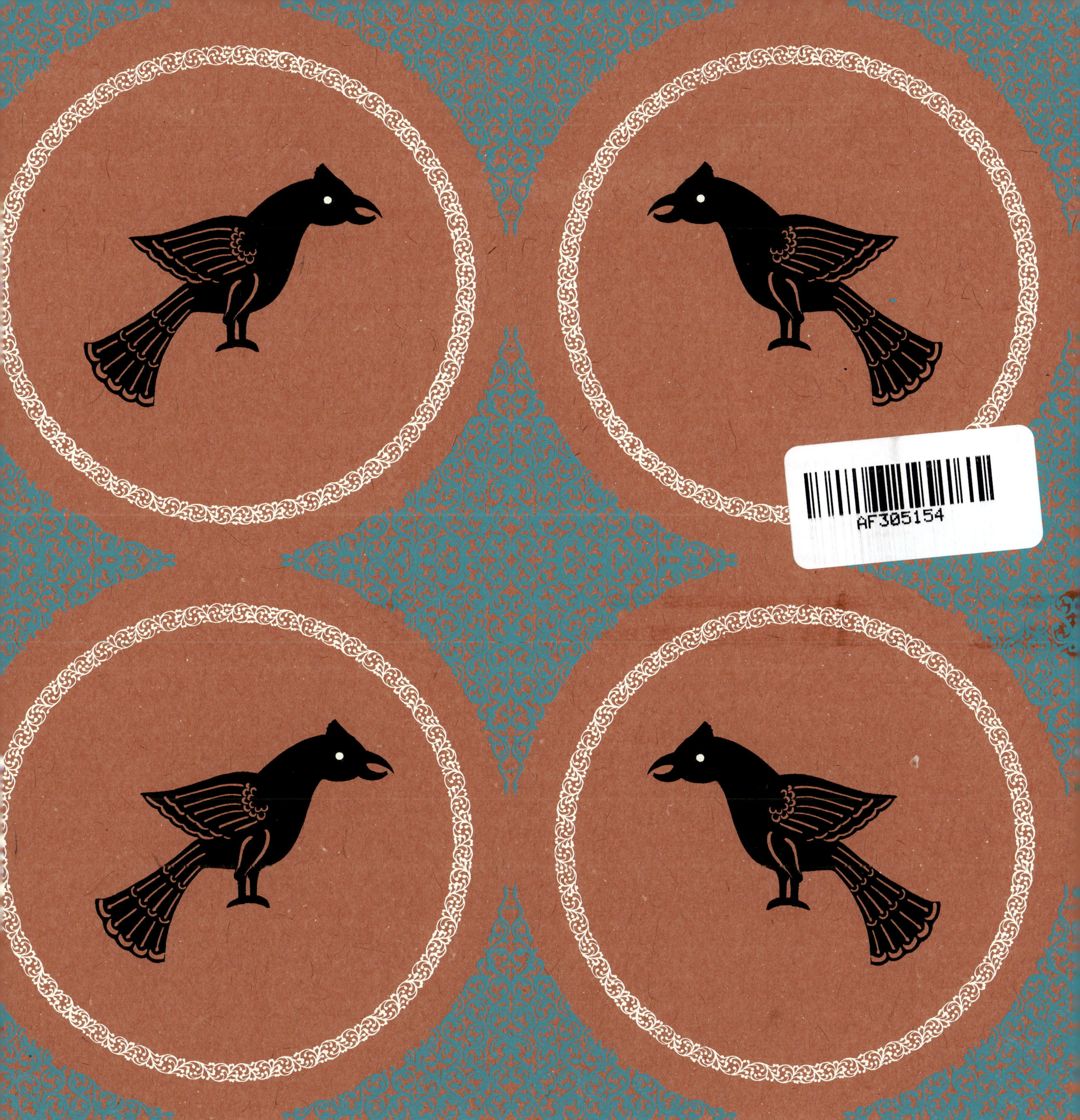
AF305154

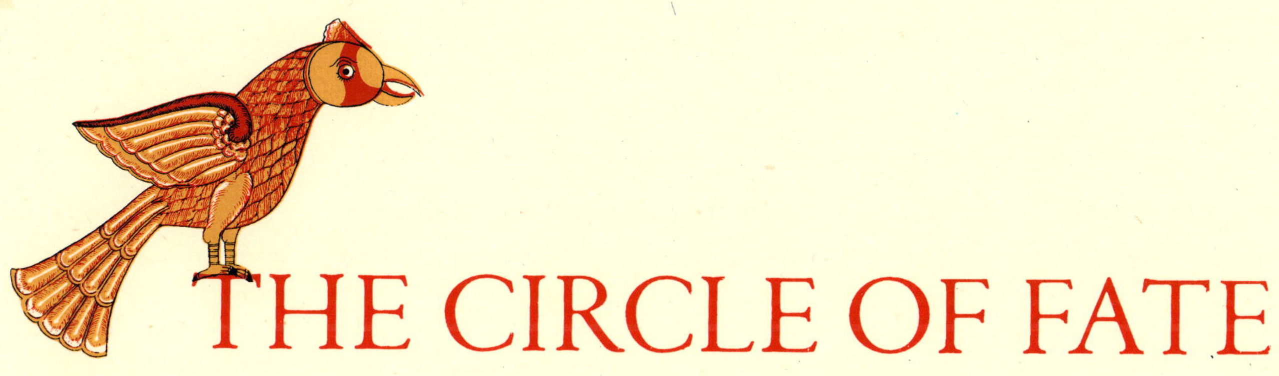

THE CIRCLE OF FATE

Art
Radhashyam Raut

Story
Raja Mohanty
Sirish Rao

TARA BOOKS

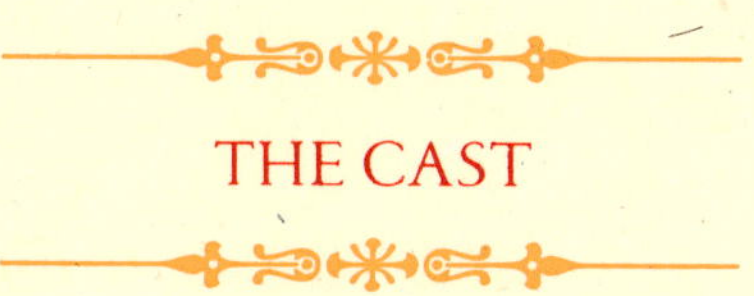

THE CAST

Lord Shiva
god of dance and destruction

Garuda
protagonist of the story,
giant bird who is the vehicle of Lord Vishnu

The snake
that lives on the tree

The beautiful little bird
that lives in the mountains

Lord Yama
god of death

The buffalo
vehicle of Lord Yama

The tree
on which the little bird sits

Lord Vishnu
preserver of the Universe

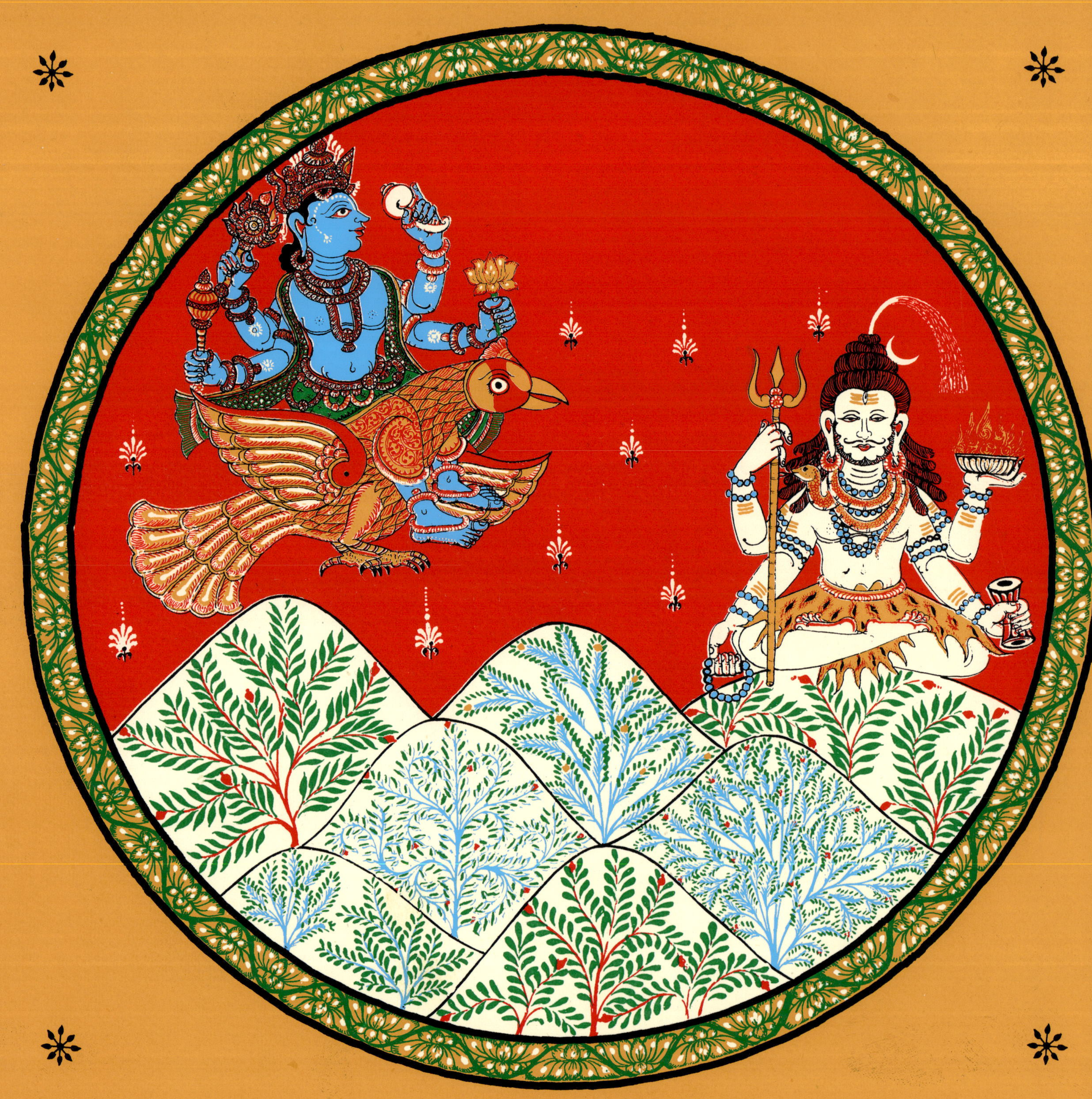

THE FLIGHT TO KAILASH

Garuda carries Lord Vishnu over the snowy peaks of the Himalaya, to Mount Kailash, home of Lord Shiva.

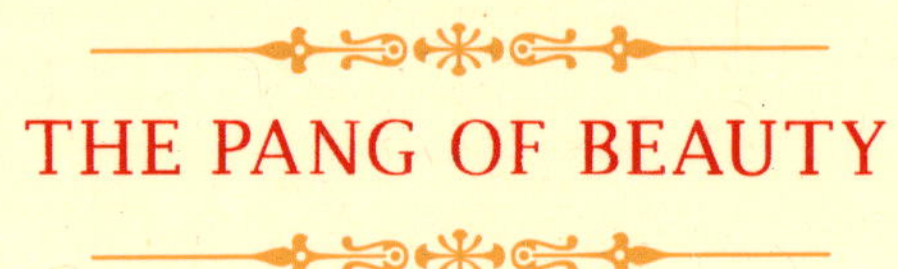

THE PANG OF BEAUTY

Garuda waits while his master visits Lord Shiva, and spots a tiny and exquisitely beautiful bird sitting on a nearby bush. He is moved by its beauty, and can scarcely believe that something like it exists.

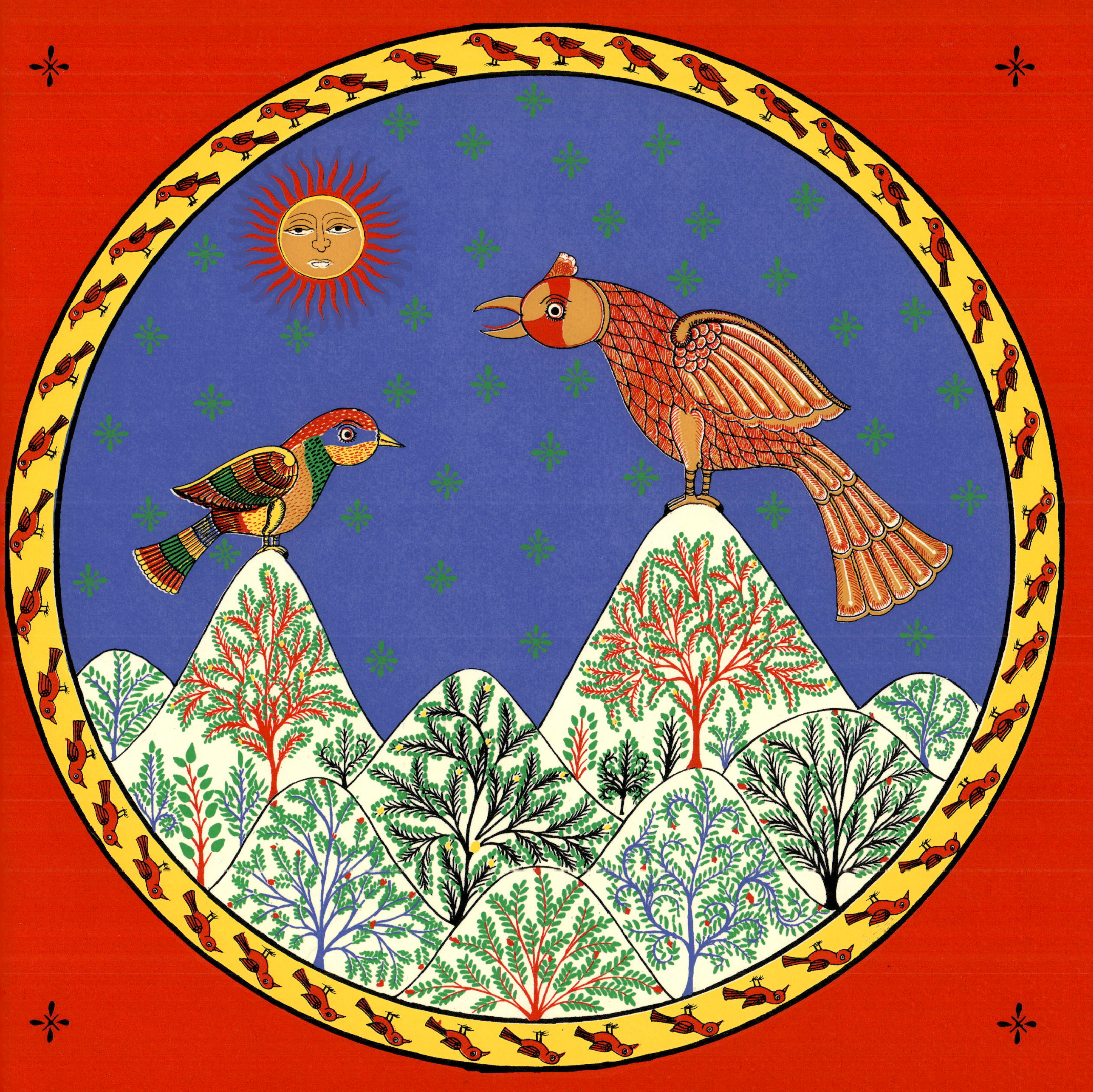

THE LOOK OF DEATH

Lord Yama, god of death, comes riding by on his buffalo. There is something wrong with his account books and he wants to clear the matter with Shiva, the god of destruction. His eyes fall on the tiny bird, and he peers at it.

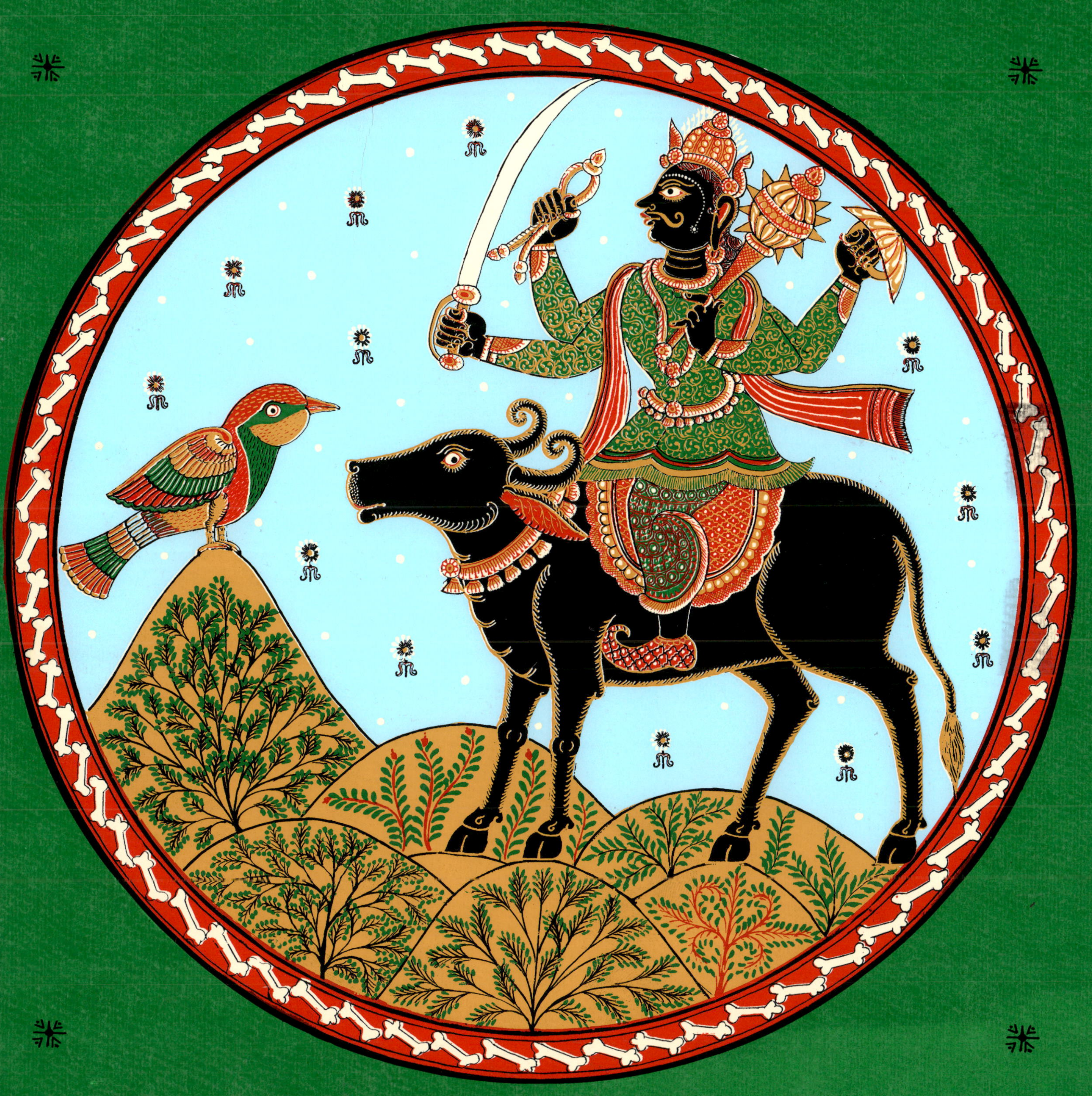

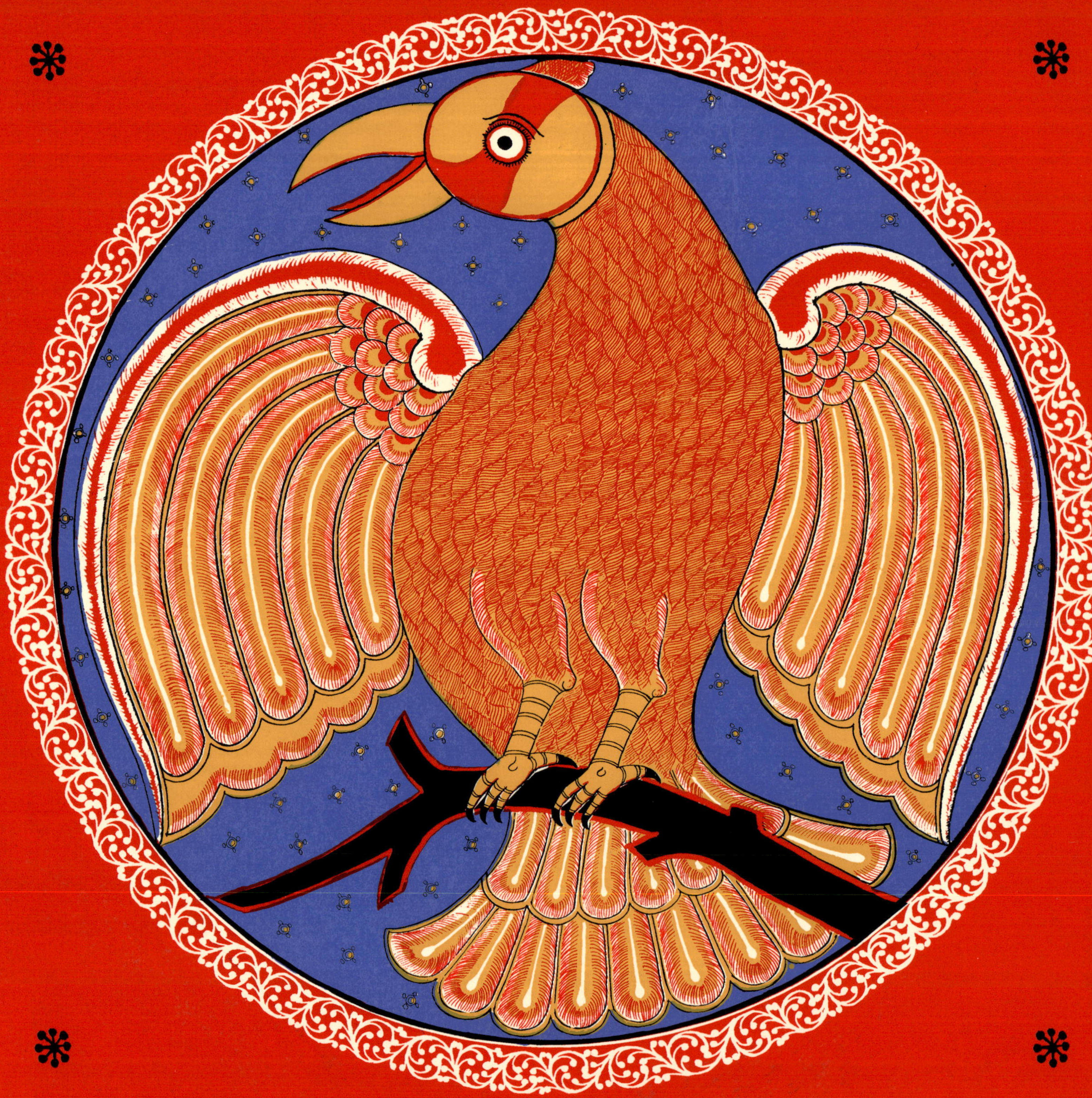

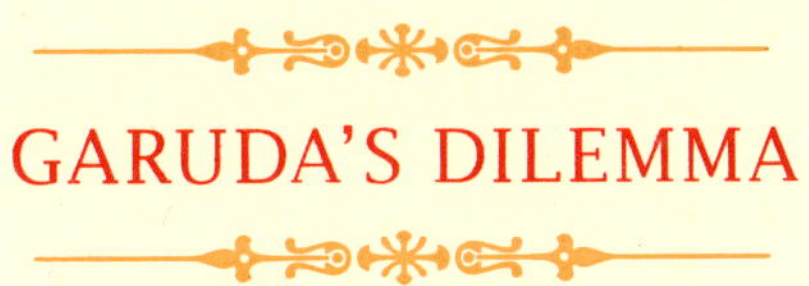

GARUDA'S DILEMMA

The look on Lord Yama's face throws Garuda into despair. 'When the god of death looks at a creature in that way,' he thinks, 'it can only mean its time has come.' He wants to save the bird from death. One part of him says it is not wise to fight the will of the gods, the other part cannot let him stand by, doing nothing. Garuda is ruffled.

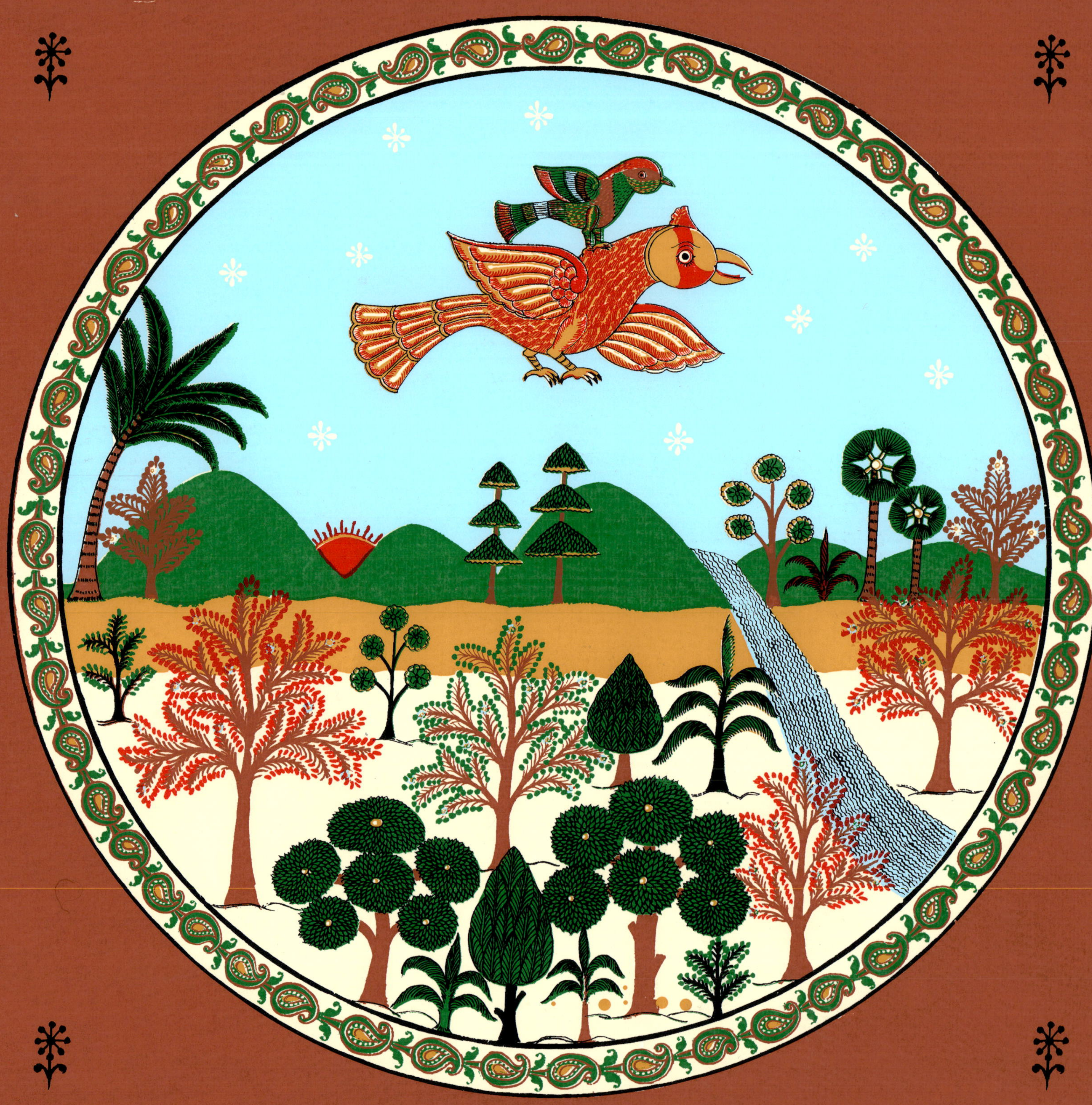

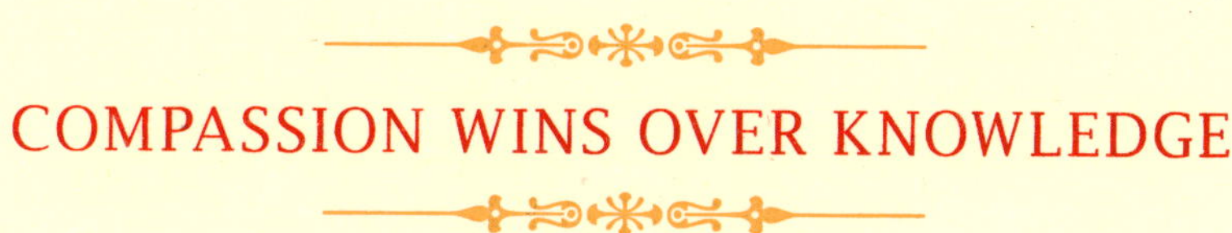

Finally the whisper of compassion triumphs over the certainty of knowledge. Garuda decides to save the bird's life, all the while begging the forgiveness of the gods. He carries the bird off to a faraway forest.

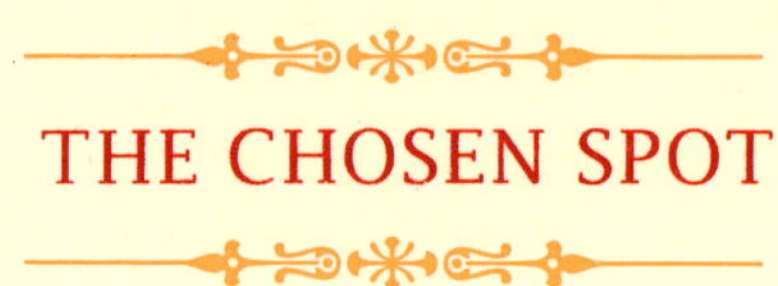

THE CHOSEN SPOT

Garuda leaves the tiny bird on a safe perch on a tree in front of a hermitage. Satisfied with a job well done, he wings his way back to the mountains.

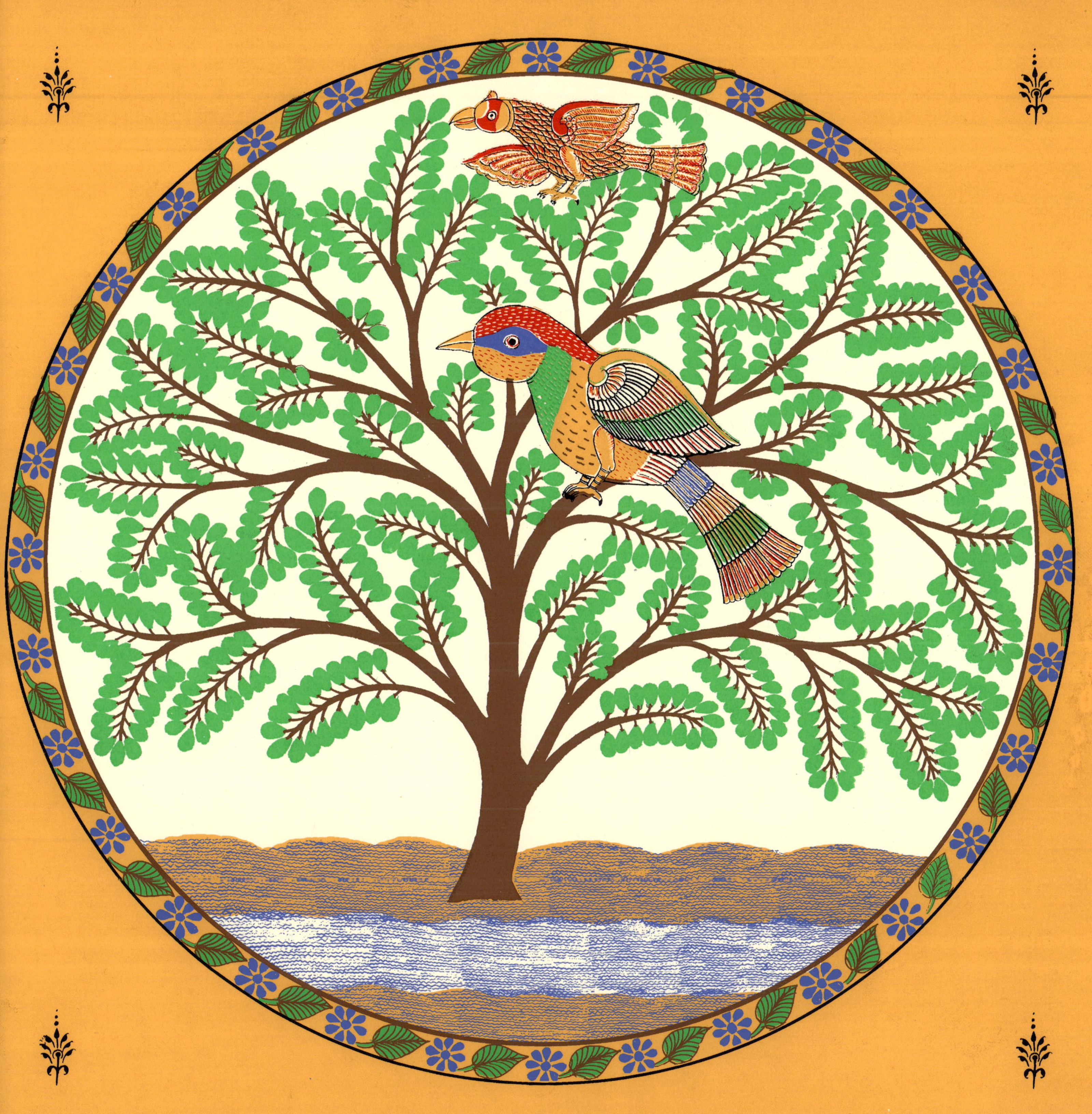

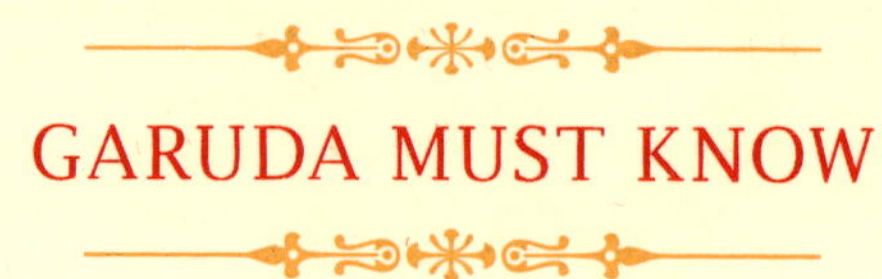

GARUDA MUST KNOW

No sooner has he landed, than Garuda meets Lord Yama, the god of death coming out of Lord Shiva's abode. Unable to bear his curiosity, he asks Yama why he looked at the tiny bird so strangely.

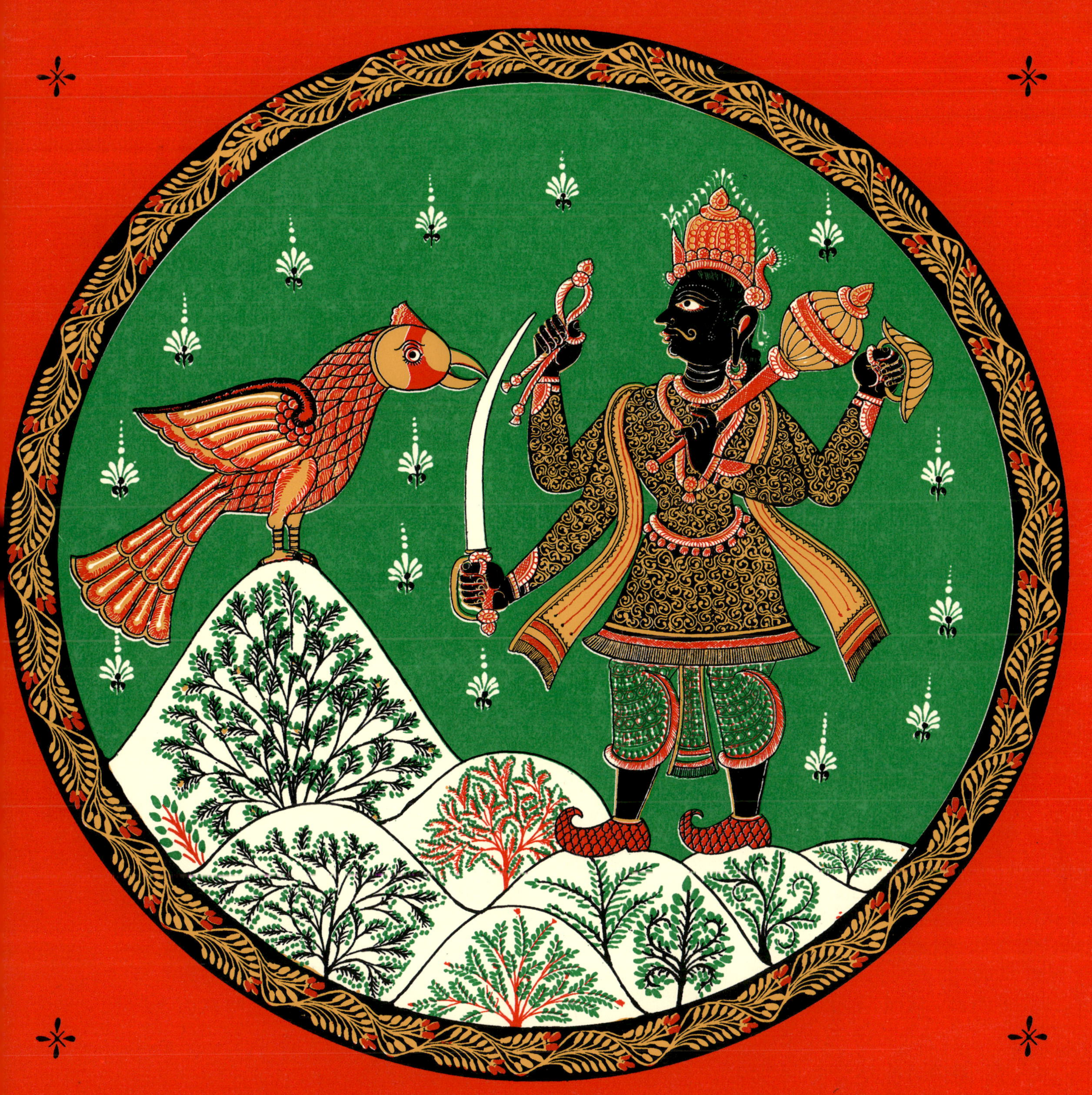

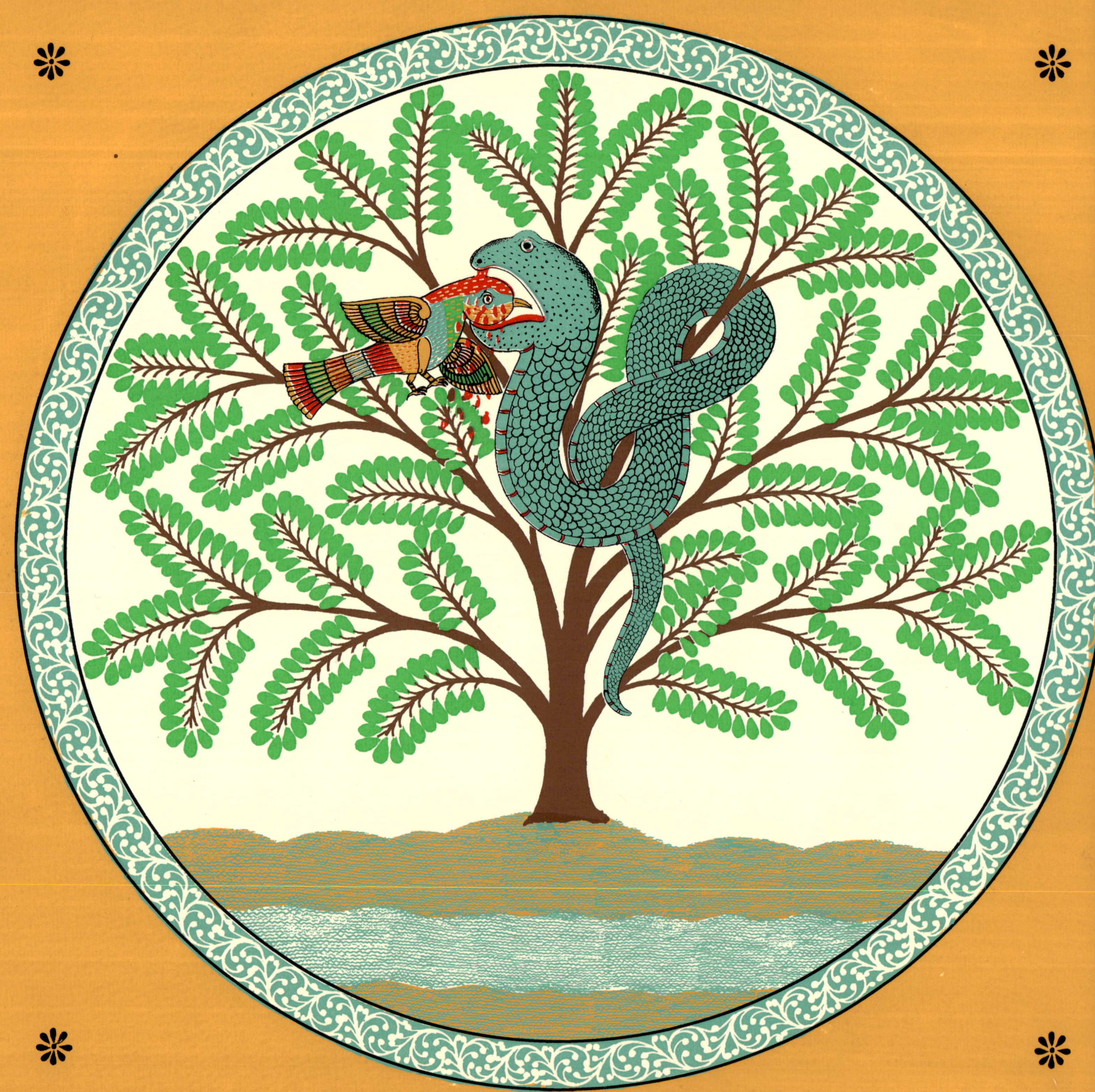

THE GOD OF DEATH ANSWERS

Yama replies that he was perplexed to see the bird near the mountains. According to his records, it was to be in a forest, on a tree near a hermitage. A python was supposed to eat it, and the bird was to be re-born in the hermitage. But since the workings of fate are above the god of death too, he left it to fate to take care of the matter.

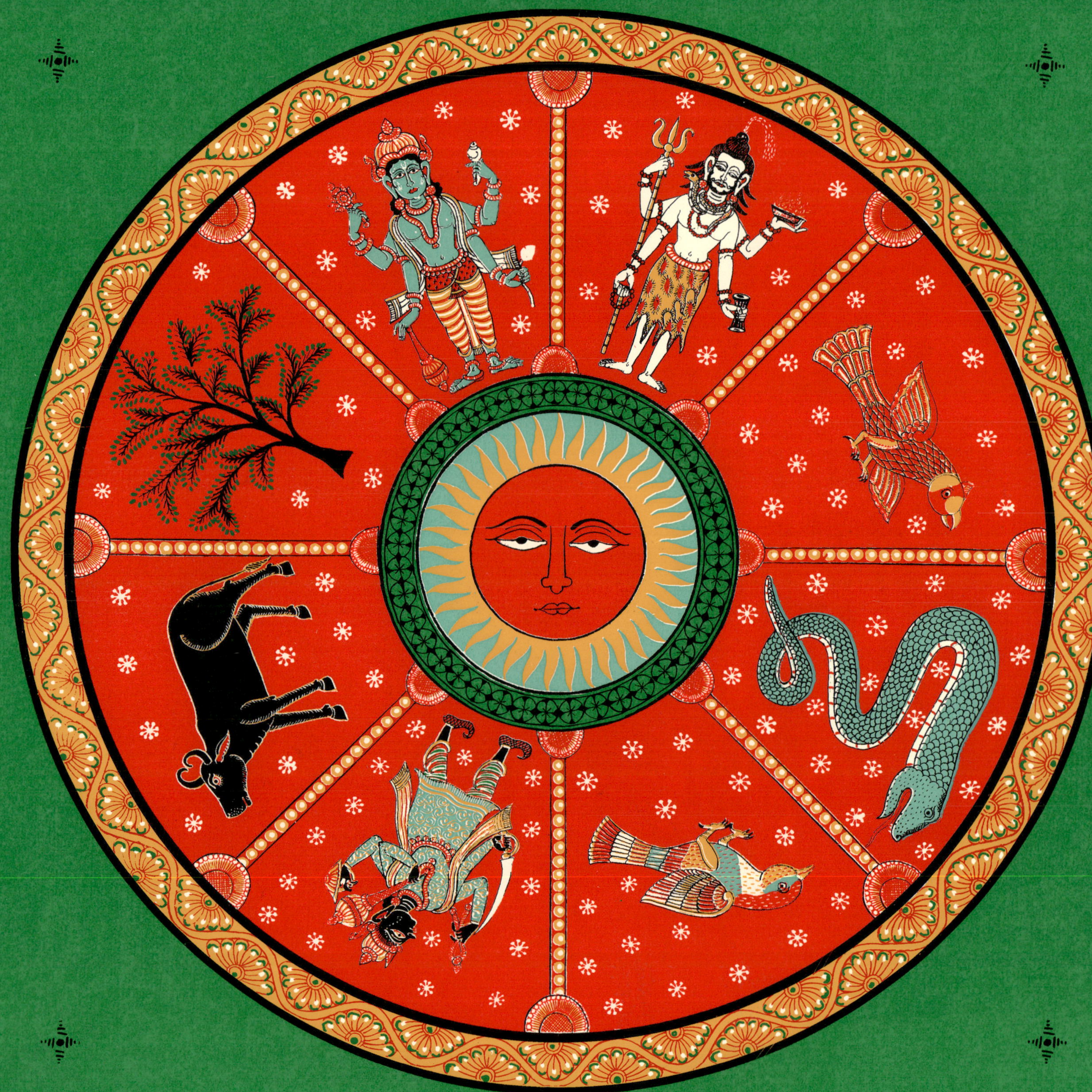

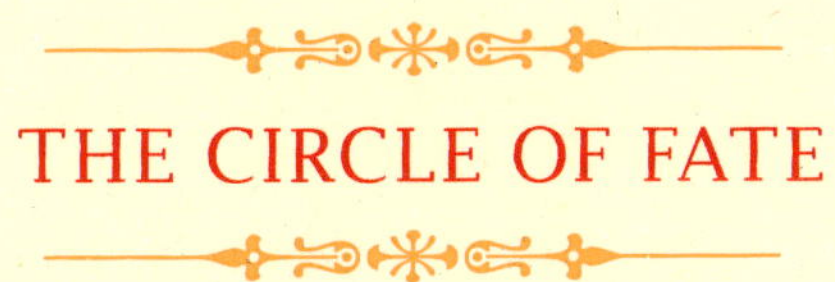

THE CIRCLE OF FATE

When Yama has gone, his words weighing like a stone in Garuda's stomach, the great bird realizes the truth.

The world is a never-ending cycle, where everything has a time and place. Even a thing of exquisite beauty must come to an end and be re-born as something else. There is a pattern. If you want to change it, you must act in the way your heart dictates. But in the end, it is you who belong in the pattern. It does not belong to you.

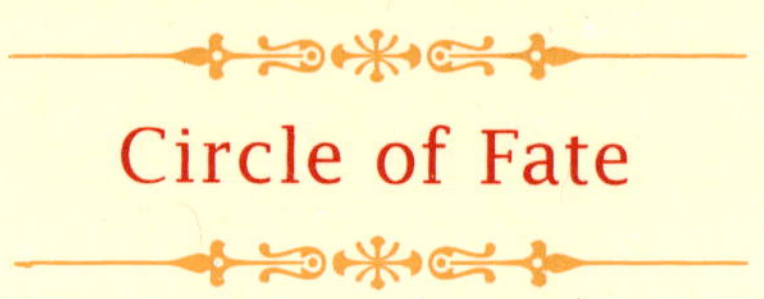

Circle of Fate

Copyright © 2019 Tara Books Pvt. Ltd.
For the text: Raja Mohanty, Sirish Rao
For the illustrations: Radhyashyam Raut

First edition 2008 | Second edition 2010

Tara Books Pvt. Ltd., India ‹www.tarabooks.com›
and
Tara Publishing Ltd., UK ‹www.tarabooks.com/uk›

Design: Rathna Ramanathan
Production: C. Arumugam

Printed by T. S. Manikandan, A. Neelagandan, K. Prabhu,
A. Arivazhagan, T. Sakthivel, R. Shanmugam, S. Mariyappan,
A. Ramesh, M. Rajesh, S. Boopalan, S. Chinraj and Ramachandran.
Bound by M. Veerasamy, M. Vinodha, M. Bhavani,
R. Selvi, V. Usha, P. Amsaveni and N. Shanthi
at AMM Screens, Chennai, India.

ISBN 978-81-86211-58-8

The authors of the book would like to acknowledge the invaluable insights provided
by the eminent writer Manoj Das, in his narrative of this ancient Indian tale; Dinanath
Pathy for his critical comments on Patachitra; IRCC, IIT Mumbai, for a seed grant for the
research project that led to this work.

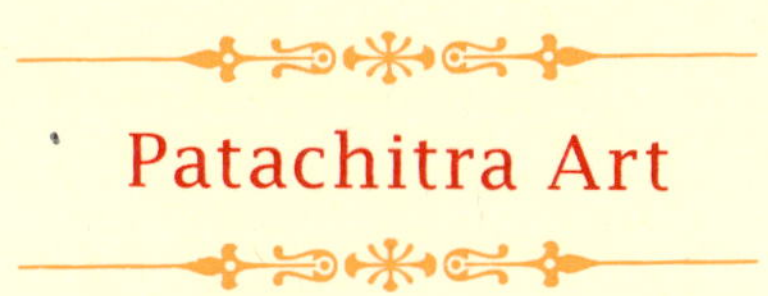

Patachitra Art

The art for this story has been especially created in the Patachitra
style from Orissa in eastern India. Patachitra means painting on canvas
– Pata is a special canvas made from cloth, and Chitra means painting.

The art started around the ancient temple of Puri in Orissa, where
artists used to paint the walls with images and stories of the local gods.
Visitors to the temple liked to take back a keepsake from their visit, and
so artists would create scrolls and cards with traditional stories and tales.
These were the first Patachitras. Over time, they also made beautiful
toys, boxes, games and masks, all painted in the Patachitra style.

There are many artists who work in the Patachitra style, and they are
part of a community. They work together in their homes, or in the
village square. Children help their parents and learn the art from them.

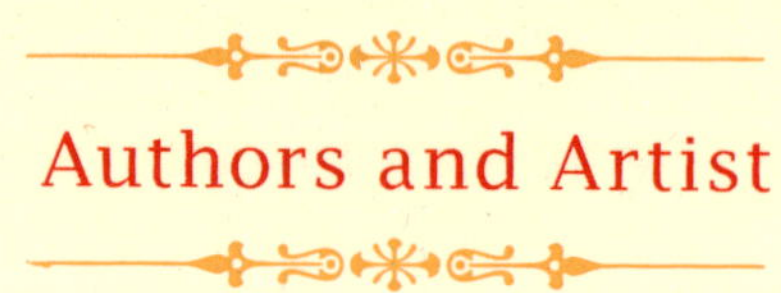

Authors and Artist

Radhashyam Raut is a young painter trained in the traditional art of Patachitra paintings of Orissa. Awarded a national scholarship, he lives and works in a village near Dhauli, the historic site of the Kalinga war after which the emperor Ashoka embraced Buddhism.

Raja Mohanty has written and illustrated ten books, many of them made by his own hand, from adaptations of Chekhov stories to 'silly tales' for children. He teaches courses in design and visual arts at the Industrial Design Centre at the IIT in Mumbai, and is involved in several projects on Indian artistic and cultural traditions.

Sirish Rao is one of the most exciting new voices in contemporary Indian writing, and has authored 16 books, ranging from novels to children's books, re-tellings of myths, and collections of pop art. His books have been translated into Dutch, Italian, French, German and Korean.

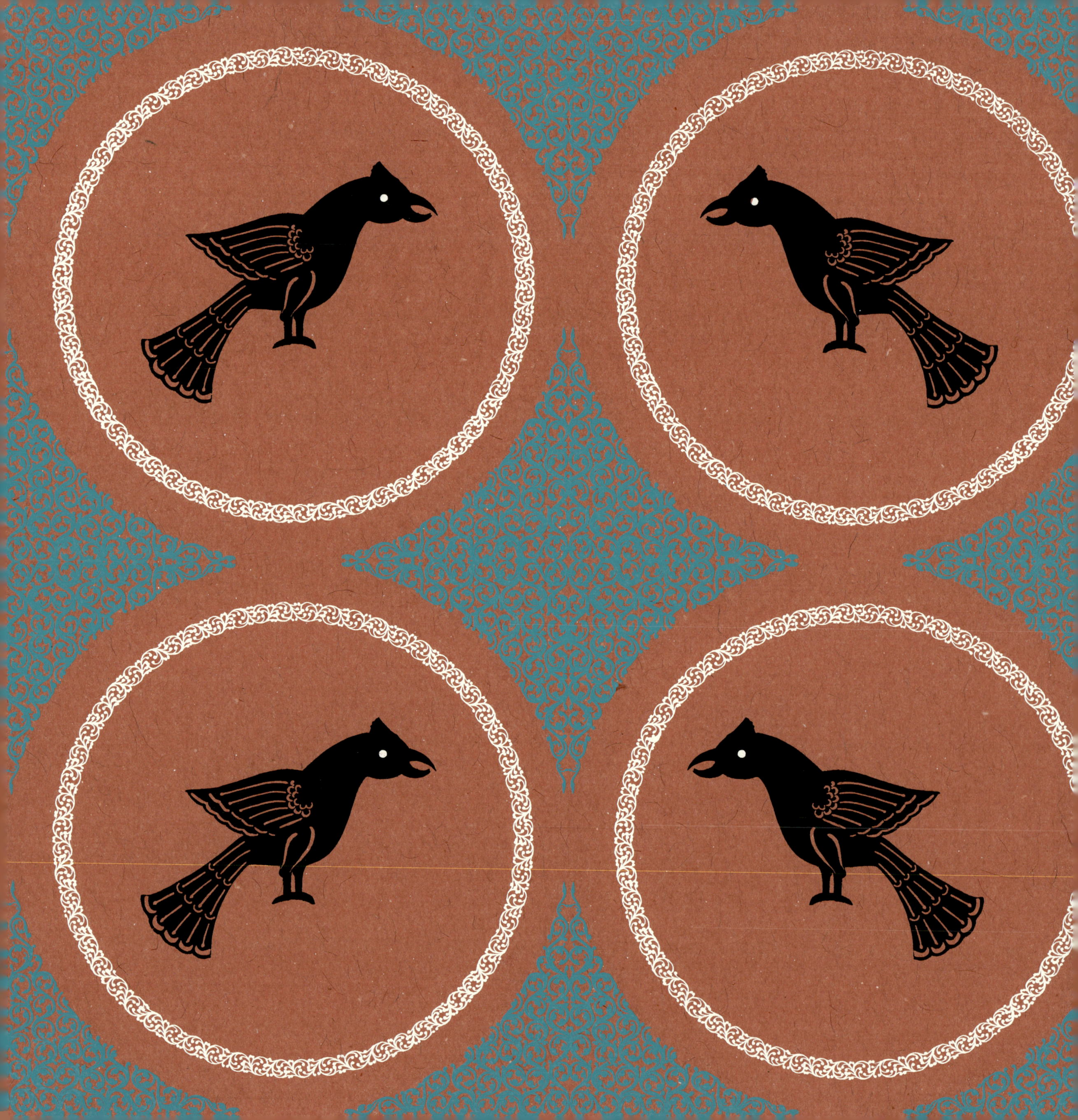